Hyenas

Children Book of Fun Facts & Amazing Photos on Animals in Nature - A Wonderful Hyenas Book for Kids aged 3-7

By

Ina Felix

Ina Felix

Copyright © 2015 by Ina Felix

All rights reserved. No part of this book may be used or reproduced in any manner whatsoever without the express written permission of the publisher except for the use of brief quotations in a book review. Image Credits: Royalty free images reproduced under license from various stock image repositories. Under a creative commons licenses.

I am a hyena.

I am a mammal like rabbits, horses, and cows.

I can be found roaming in Africa.

I live in the hot savanna, where there are grass and very few trees.

I am a carnivore like lions, wolves, and tigers.

I hunt for food together with my fellow hyenas.

I love to eat meat like other predators.

I can run very fast when chasing and catching prey.

Hyenas

My favorite preys are wildebeest, antelopes, and zebras.

Sometimes, I hunt smaller prey like birds, lizards, and snakes.

Hyenas

I make a very noisy sound when hunting.

It sounds like I am laughing.

I can bite very hard with my powerful jaws.

I sometimes eat food left behind by other predators.

I am very territorial just like other predators.

Hyenas

My fellow hyenas and I protect our territory by from lions, wild dogs, and leopards.

Our fur is mostly colored brown but some of us have reddish coats.

I had several spots when I was young.

My spots disappeared as I grew older.

Hyenas

I can have many children.

I train my children to hunt and look for food just like our elders.

Hyenas

I hope you had fun learning about my family.

Thank you.

Made in the USA
Middletown, DE
29 November 2016